PORTFOLIO J

METROPOLITAN SEMINARS IN ART

Great Periods in Painting

PORTFOLIO J

Summer Idyl: THE FLOWERING OF IMPRESSIONISM

BY JOHN CANADAY

ART EDITOR AND CRITIC
THE NEW YORK TIMES

THE METROPOLITAN MUSEUM OF ART

SUMMER IDYL

The Flowering of Impressionism

IN 1870 the painter Henri Fantin-Latour (1836–1904) paid homage to his friend Édouard Manet in a picture called *A Studio in the Batignolles Quarter* (*Figure 1*). The time was seven years after the Salon des Refusés, with its scandal of *The Picnic*, and only five years after the greater scandal of *Olympia*. Manet, now thirty-eight, was the most talked-of artist in France, although he had sold fewer than half a dozen pictures. He had succeeded Courbet as the symbol of the artist's independence, and a group of painters, writers, and dilettantes had formed around his table at the Café Guerbois, the successor to Courbet's Brasserie des Martyrs. Among them were the young artists who a few years later were to be known as impressionists.

Fantin-Latour, a respected and relatively conservative artist, was sympathetic to the work of these men, but he remained on the fringe of the group without participating actively in its revolt. The almost photographic realism of pictures like *A Studio in the Batignolles Quarter* made him acceptable to the Salon and its public, since his realism was unassociated with Courbet's so-called socialism or Manet's heresies of technique.

Manet is at his easel. Seated next to him is Zacharie Astruc, a writer (and a painter of sorts) who had defended Manet during the Salon des Refusés and who was to continue as a spokesman for the impressionists. Standing at Astruc's side is Émile Zola whose realistic novels and political editorials, and particularly whose denunciations of the government in 1898 for its part in the Dreyfus Affair, were to make him one of the great social forces in his country. Zola had written about Manet, prophesying that he would eventually find his place in the Louvre. Near Zola, his head framed by the picture on the wall, is a young painter, Pierre Auguste Renoir (1841–1919). His friend Jean Frédéric Bazille, tall and handsome, stands at the right. Bazille, a painter Renoir's age and as promising, was killed the same year, 1870, in the battle of Beaune-la-Rolande in the Franco-Prussian War. The shadowy face behind Bazille is that of another painter whose name most people know, Claude Monet (1840–1926). (The confusion of the name Monet with Manet was a source of intense irritation to the painter of *Olympia*.) Standing behind Manet is the only personality in the group whose name has decreased in importance or interest. He is Otto Scholderer, a friend of both Manet and Fantin-Latour who worked successfully enough in Paris and London. The eighth portrait is of Edmond Maître, an amateur musician who appears frequently in his friends' paintings.

Certainly all these men look well disposed and gentle enough. Yet during the following years they were to be accused of undermining the great tradition of France, of being subversives, madmen, frauds, incompetents, and degenerates—all on the score of paintings that are today widely loved and admired throughout the western world.

5

Figure 1

When Fantin painted *A Studio in the Batig-nolles Quarter* the idea of organizing a society to exhibit outside the Salon was already germinating in the minds of the artists. The group was formed in 1874. Their first exhibition was given under the noncommittal name *Société anonyme des artistes peintres, sculptures, graveurs, etc.* The name did not last long because a better one evolved during the exhibition. One of the 165 pictures in the show, a canvas by Monet, was called *Impression: Sunrise.* It was considered a hilarious painting and a hilarious title by members of the public who came to scoff at the new art. The painters were dubbed "impressionists" as a joke, but they recognized the appropriateness of the word and before long changed the name of their society to Peintres Impressionistes.

Altogether the impressionists held eight ex-hibitions before the society disbanded, the first in 1874 and the last in 1886, with many changes in membership over the years. The kind of pictures exhibited changed too, for even the founding members soon became dis-satisfied with impressionist ideas and, with the explorative spirit that has characterized art since their time, set about experimenting.

Impressionism and Light

Just what is impressionism? Let us say first that the term should never be misused to iden-tify just any painting that is broad and free in execution. The impressionists themselves never reached a precise definition of the word, al-though one suggested was "painting in terms of tone rather than in terms of the object it-self." By this definition, Velazquez is a precursor of impressionism, as we have seen in his *Venus and Cupid* (Portfolio F, *Figure 8*). Any satisfactory definition must include the idea that the impressionist seeks to reproduce the effect of the light reflected on the retina of the eye from an object, rather than to reproduce the forms of the objects themselves; but impressionism also included a theory of color. Claude Monet most persistently investigated this theory.

Monet once said that he wished he could have been born blind and then have been given his sight in order to see and paint in terms of pure light without previous knowledge of the forms over which it played. In his *Île aux Fleurs* (Plate J1) he comes about as close to painting in this way as anyone has ever done. The trees across the river appear to his eye not as tree forms but as bits of bluish and greenish color. Trying to eliminate from his consciousness the foreknowledge that these are objects of a certain familiar shape composed of smaller objects of certain other familiar shapes, he applies his color in dots and dabs approximating tonality and general shape as they are visible through intervening distance with its specific kind and degree of light and atmosphere. The light from the water reaches his eye as a sparkle of broken tints, so he paints it as such. Courbet would have tried to re-create the weight, the texture, and the flow that he knew was the nature of water as a body of matter, rather than merely the reflecting surface.

The objects at closer range, the flowering shrubs and grasses of the immediate foreground, are seen as clusters, sprinklings, spots, small streaks, and speckles of color. A stem or a leaf or a blossom seems identifiable because the shape of a fleck or a broken line of light approximates the shape of the form as we know it. From our own foreknowledge we supply unconsciously much of the detail that Monet so carefully avoided reproducing.

Compositionally this approach to painting implies random effects, a glimpse of some transient aspect of nature organized only by the artist's selection of a scene that has a degree of inherent balance and organization. The eye being only a kind of camera responding to light and the canvas being only a kind of film upon which the light images are projected, the usual process of selective organization is, at best, limited. Recognizing this limitation, one of Monet's friends said that he was "only an eye." But, recognizing also the beauty of Monet's work, he added, "—but what an eye!"

We are so familiar with so many thousand paintings of this general kind that we find nothing bizarre in the technique that horrified our grandfathers. On the contrary it has become such a common practice of landscapists that most amateurs try to approximate it, often in inconsistent and disharmonious ways, and the most tiresomely repetitious artists imitate it. In the hands of such a master as Monet this way of painting is the ultimate visual realism, recognizing finally the logical relationship between the eye and the world: a relationship of light. Velazquez had recognized the same relationship, most effectively in his interiors; but the impressionists were mainly preoccupied with the light of out-of-doors and with ways of approximating the vibration of light as well as its color.

In nature this vibration is a blending of the components of the spectrum—red, orange, yellow, green, blue, and violet. It is lost in translating the effects of light into paint in the usual ways. The impressionists hoped to bring paint and light into identity with one another by eliminating from the palette all browns, blacks, grays, and colors other than those of the spectrum and by applying the spectrum colors in vivacious strokes, juxtaposed, leaving them to be blended by the eye instead of mixing them beforehand. At least this was the basis of their theory. They seldom held to it strictly, but we can find examples where an area of green foliage, for instance, may be composed of bits of true green, blue-green, yellow-green, even pure blue and pure yellow.

Intermingled, they make an over-all green that conventional painters would have mixed on the palette.

At other times the swarming colors of impressionism may shift and change so rapidly that they are unidentifiable as a color mass. What color are the foreground bushes in *Île aux Fleurs*? We cannot say, yet the eye receives the impression of flowering bushes, vibrant in light and air. Delacroix had hinted at impressionist theory, and practice, when he defined color as "a merging of reflections," the germ of the impressionist idea that color is a fusion of many colors. He gave the name *flochetage* to his technique of applying colors in individual strokes, although he did not develop the impressionist idea of using the eye as a kind of prism to break color into its component parts. Nineteenth-century scientific research by such men as Chevreul, Helmholtz, Maxwell, and Rood into the nature of light and color may have influenced the impressionists somewhat, but we must not exaggerate the scientific aspects of their theories, which were not precisely formulated. The painters continued to trust their eyes first, while working on the general principle we have just described.

Boudin and Daubigny

In his early development Monet was much influenced by Eugène Louis Boudin (1824–1898). This painter, sixteen years older than Monet, had taken a friendly interest in the Le Havre youth who was intent upon becoming a painter in spite of the objections of his parents and who was trying to pick up a little money here and there doing caricatures. Boudin was one of many landscape painters who used to do beach scenes and marines at various spots along the coast. In recent years his small, beautifully painted pictures have become increasingly popular, partly because his importance as an impressionist has been recognized and partly because the pictures themselves are so attractive. *Approaching Storm* (Plate J 2)

is Boudin at his typical best, with its low horizon, its strip of beach peopled with seated and strolling figures, its bright spots of red, yellow, blue, and white in hats and dresses played against deep water and sky. The formula never palls as Boudin uses it. Impressionism was inherent in his approach to painting, and he exhibited with the younger men when the society was formed. Boudin also did views of the rural countryside, much in the Barbizon spirit but with the more high-keyed impressionist palette.

The Barbizon painters themselves made an important contribution to impressionism when they discovered that the least exotic landscape might yield subject matter and, above all, when they began to paint in the presence of nature, even though they might only make sketches in this way for pictures to be worked up in the studio. Of all the Barbizon men, Charles François Daubigny (1817–1878) is most notable as a protoimpressionist because he insisted on painting as much as possible out of doors and because he was importantly associated with the young Monet.

Twenty-three years older than Monet, Daubigny was sharing the success of the Barbizon school of painters while Monet was struggling through his extremely difficult early days of poverty. Daubigny befriended the younger man, and on occasion they painted together. Daubigny had rigged up a kind of miniature floating studio, building a protective canopy over a rowboat in order to station himself at the best points for his favorite subject, a farmhouse or two on low banks seen across a body of quiet water in the foreground. *Evening* (Plate J 3), or at least studies for it, must have been painted from this boat, which Monet later on was to use as the model for a floating studio of his own.

Daubigny loved gentle, sometimes misty air and subdued light; in a most inconspicuous way he anticipated impressionism by juxtaposing strokes of color instead of blending them and by eliminating details in a somewhat

Figure 2

impressionist regard for effects of light. His departures from convention are so mild, however, that it is surprising to discover that he was attacked for them and that the derisive word "impression" was applied to his work years before it was adapted as a label for a school. Certainly the poetic *Evening* is a study in solid forms more closely related, in our eyes, to a Chardin still life than to the sparkling—and disintegrating—forms of impressionism.

Form and Impressionism

This disintegration of form is apparent, but not disturbing, in Monet's *Île aux Fleurs*. In his later work, however, solid forms completely dissolve in a shimmer of light effects, as for instance in a series of studies he made of Rouen Cathedral, one of which is here illustrated (*Figure 2*); and to this extreme some members of the impressionist group were unwilling to follow him.

The cathedral series, like one of haystacks and another of poplar trees, was a programmatic demonstration of Monet's theories about the painting of light. He painted the structure in morning light, full daylight, evening light; on dull days, rainy days, and sunny days. But we might argue that, in truth, he never painted the cathedral at all. The stone becomes cotton fluff bathed in pink, blue, and lavender iridescence, a soft opalescent shimmer. By standards of formal composition, the building is placed as carelessly as it might be in a snapshot by an unskilled tourist.

The picture may be regarded in several ways. As a didactic demonstration it loses interest as a work of art. As an almost abstract pattern of color it has an unexpected relationship to contemporary art (in this connection we will encounter Monet in a later discussion). But as a picture of a cathedral the painting is a mangling of architectural forms. This aspect of impressionism, no doubt, was the one that led Corot, usually the gentlest and most tolerant of men, to call the impressionists "that gang."

Figure 3

Pissarro

The only painter who might compete with Monet for the title of the purest impressionist is Camille Pissarro (1830–1903), who arrived in Paris in 1855, the year of the great Exposition and of Courbet's Pavilion of Realism. In the history of the impressionist group, Pissarro, a man slightly older than his colleagues, emerges as a saint. He encouraged the younger men, helped them financially in spite of his own limited means and large family, and finally advised and helped a still younger group, the postimpressionists, when they in turn were fighting for existence and recognition.

To write at length about Pissarro's career would be to repeat much that we have said about Monet's except that, unlike Monet, Pissarro reached a point where he could no longer watch buildings, trees, and people dissolving into a tinted mist. He began to see impressionism as a dangerous path or at best a blind alley, and he joined a group of reformers, the "neoimpressionists." Neoimpressionism was an effort to retain the luminosity of impressionism by retaining the idea of color divided into its component parts; but it added the idea of calculating the proportions of the parts as scientifically as possible and applying the pigment in tiny uniform dots. We will be reading more of this development in our next discussion.

But if impressionism had become too loose and undirected a technique to please Pissarro, he found neoimpressionism, on the other hand, frigid and restricting. Abandoning it, he reverted to more vivacious color and brushwork, and thus arrived at a form of chastened impressionism exemplified in *The Pont Neuf*

(Plate J4), painted in 1901, two years before his death at seventy-three. If the bit of the Seine filling the lower right corner is compared with the water in Monet's *Île aux Fleurs*, we can see how Pissarro disciplined his brush without cramping it. The crowds and the vehicles on the bridge are the still recognizable descendants of Boudin's strollers and beach cabins; the buildings in the background and the stone piers of the bridge are solid in spite of their being conceived as objects seen through intervening atmosphere; the engaging informality of snapshot composition enlivens an arrangement also carefully considered as an entity.

Renoir: Early Works

The first member of the founding group to become dissatisfied with impressionism was Renoir. Essentially a traditionalist, his prob-

Figure 4

11

lem was to find himself as a modern French-man continuing the past without imitating its forms.

All his life Renoir held a special fondness for Boucher's pretty pictures. "Pretty," he always said, was not a word to be afraid of. But it was not the mere prettiness, it was the happy spirit of eighteenth-century court art that attracted Renoir. He was a joyous painter, and for him all the joy of life centered in woman as a symbol of the delight of the world.

One of the earliest Renoirs we have (he destroyed a body of earlier work of a romantic type) is the *Bather with Griffon* (*Figure 3*) of 1870, the year of Fantin-Latour's group por-trait. The influence of Courbet, who was just

at the end of his career, is apparent; the figure is as opulent and the pigment as rich as any Courbet, but the color is fresher, the mood more tender, and the still life of discarded gar-ments and the little dog are painted with a lightness already hinting at impressionism. If the picture lacks anything, it is the decisive individuality of style that distinguishes the work of a great artist from that of an excellent and sensitive painter.

Success by way of the Salon was Renoir's goal from the first, not because he admired the typical Salon product, but because he had no intention of spending his life in poverty. A Salon career was the most direct route to at-tention and to the kind of prices that would

Figure 5

Figure 6

support him as a professional artist. But he was also interested in exploring effects of light and air and had already begun to do so with Monet while he was at work on *Bather with Griffon*. His work was conspicuous in the first three group shows, but he would have nothing to do with the idea held by some of the members, that all should pledge themselves not to submit to the Salon jury. He continued to submit, with frequent acceptances, until a contract with the dealer Durand-Ruel gave him financial independence.

For the third impressionist exhibition, 1877, Renoir painted an ambitious show piece, the now celebrated *Dancing at the Moulin de la Galette* (*Figure 4*). This is an impressionist demonstration of shifting lights and dappled prismatic shadows, and its subject holds to the impressionist tenet that a painting should be a glimpse of a momentary aspect of a scene, as if caught by accident. But the picture is also a studio piece, as carefully worked out as any Salon painting. In addition it is a subject picture, a picture of courtship that goes beneath the surface representation of attractive young men and women at a dance. Without obvious idealization, and always with reference to the contemporary and the commonplace, *Moulin de la Galette* is nevertheless a counterpart of Watteau's *Embarkation for Cythera* (Plate G 2) expressed in terms acceptable to a painter in a century that put its faith primarily in bourgeois standards.

Technically, Renoir's impressionism differs from Monet's in an important way. For Monet color was a phenomenon to be investigated and explained by demonstration; for Renoir it was an aesthetic principle. Or, put another way, Monet was a color theorist and Renoir was a colorist. He is in a direct line from Rubens through Watteau and Delacroix. If we compare Renoir's picture of *Monet Painting*

Figure 7

in His Garden in Argenteuil (Plate J 5) with Monet's *Île aux Fleurs* or Pissarro's *Pont Neuf* we may find similarities in the use of broken color. In varying degrees the forms tend to fuse with light in the same way. But Renoir's color, as color, has its own harmonies; its intensities are beyond those of nature. Where Monet and Pissarro approximate the sparkle of light in a normal world, Renoir creates a glowing world that is a personal vision, in spite of its origin in a purely optical one. It is as if some dulling film has been stripped from our eyes to show us colors not only more intense than those we ordinarily see but also closer to some inner life that accounts for them.

Renoir: Return to Tradition

Renoir was finding patrons by the late 1870s, and in 1878 Madame Charpentier, the wife of an influential publisher, commissioned him to do her portrait with her two little daughters (*Figure 5*). Here Renoir modified his impressionist technique, tightening it somewhat, for the double reason that he wanted the picture to be a Salon success, which it was in 1879, and that he was becoming more and more dissatisfied with the light touch of impressionism, which he thought was ending in monotony and repetition. He refused to exhibit in three group shows in a row.

He could have turned himself into a sound but still commercially successful painter at this time had he wished to continue along the lines of the Charpentier portrait. But he remained always an artist who thought first of his work, hoping for success through it, and only secondarily of success itself. Restless and dissatisfied, saying that as an impressionist he was forgetting "how to paint and to draw," he gathered together his available funds for a trip to Italy in 1882, with the idea of finding himself through contact with the art of the Renaissance.

His immediate goal was Raphael's series of frescoes in the Vatican (Portfolio 8, *Figure 10*;

Figure 8

Portfolio E, *Figures 2* and *3*). He found in them the grandeur and the nobility he had hoped for. By chance he also hit upon an early treatise on painting, the late fourteenth-century handbook on the painter's craft by Cennino Cennini, a follower of Giotto. The tempera techniques described in it (outlined in Portfolio 9) demanded a care and precision directly opposed to the freedom and suggestion of impressionism. The book supported Renoir's conviction that he needed the discipline of the most demanding craftsmanship. He did not make the mistake of turning to fresco or to tempera, there being no justification for such an extreme, but he did return to the craftsmanlike formal definition of the early masters. Back in France, he chose as a test

15

piece a standard Salon subject, bathers in a landscape. This was his most ambitious picture since *Moulin de la Galette* and an exercise in the organization of forms sharply defined, tightly modeled, and arbitrarily composed. (The portrait of Madame Renoir, Plate 3 in Portfolio 1, with its emphasis on geometrical construction, belongs to the same period.)

Renoir worked on the *Bathers* (*Figure 6*) for three years, from 1884 to 1887. It was a success upon exhibition in a commercial gallery, but it is in some ways a curiously inconsistent painting. Our color detail (Plate J 6), just under actual size, shows the exquisitely controlled modeling, the virtually invisible gradations, the implacably closed contours of the figures. The eye, as a particularly revealing bit, is a linear pattern as carefully studied as any by Ingres, and even the lashes are sharply represented. Yet the background, while also smooth of surface, is painted in broader, prismatic, unblended areas still related to impressionist vibrance. Compositionally, Renoir makes a point of obvious artifice as opposed to impressionism's slice-of-life realism.

Renoir leaves us in no doubt, as we stand facing the *Bathers*, that we are in the presence of a set piece, a studio demonstration of an essentially academic kind, as conscientiously executed, and executed with as much reference to the standards of the past as any competition picture by an aspirant to the Prix de Rome. The difference is that painter and master are in this case the same man who, having matured in one manner, is building upon experience and understanding to train himself in another.

Renoir: Later Periods

Renoir's four periods as a painter correspond to stages in his life, as might be expected when the work of an artist is born of his intimate response to the world. The first period with the *Moulin de la Galette* is the image of Renoir's youth; the second with the *Bathers*

is his recognition of maturity, a stock taking for the future; the third with pictures like *Two Girls at the Piano* (*Figure 7*) brings him into the full stream of his life, a time of fulfillment. At first glance *Two Girls at the Piano* (or another typical picture of the third period, which we have already seen, *In the Meadow*, Portfolio 1, Plate 4) seems a reversion to impressionism, since the forms are again softened, the mood again tender and relaxed in comparison with the formality of the *Bathers*. But if it is compared with *Moulin de la Galette*, its greater solidity is apparent. Through the three pictures runs a compositional motif dear to Renoir, an encircling or embracing gesture binding figures together. In *Moulin de la Galette* it unites a girl seated on a bench with one standing behind her and bending forward. In the *Bathers* it is varied and made the crux of the composition as the central figure spreads a cape or towel to create a nichelike enclosure; in *Two Girls at the Piano* the entire scheme is built upon it. The casual subject, affectionately treated, takes on importance because its forms are built into one another with all the self-containment and compactness of sculpture.

Renoir's fourth and final period is his least attractive to most people, yet it is his summation. By itself, a *Bather* (*Figure 8*), painted in 1917 or 1918, a year or two before Renoir's death, could seem a monstrous image. But we have reached here the reasonable conclusion to a concept that began with the *Bather with Griffon*. The swelling forms, indivisibly united with the radiant background of nature bursting with fertility, are Renoir's final expression of the joyousness and richness of life, with women, children, and nature as its symbols.

Degas

In the *Bather* Renoir can hardly be called impressionist. The color, although applied in prismatic splinters, is only remotely related to impressionism's approximation of true outdoor effects, and the subject, an ideal one, has nothing to do with impressionism's other major facet, the slice-of-life, the snapshot composition, the objective and apparently random framing of a bit of the routine world. The master of this kind of pictorial arrangement was Edgar Degas (1834–1917), but there was never an artist whose composition was less random than his. His "random" effects are the result of exquisite adjustments.

In the course of our discussions we have already seen a great deal of Degas. We compared his *Woman with Chrysanthemums* (Portfolio 1, Plate 5), as a study of personality, with Renoir's portrait of his wife; we analyzed his *Bellelli Family* (Portfolio 7, Plate 75) as a picture whose composition revealed the emotional interrelationships among four people;

we saw his *Rehearsal in the Foyer of the Opera* (Portfolio 7, Plate 77) as a snapshot composition adjusted into classical balance. *The Toilet* (Portfolio 10, Plates 114 and 115) showed us Degas as a pastelist, and we could have commented also that it represents one pole of Degas's compositional range and the formality of *The Bellelli Family* the other.

Without repeating our discussions of these pictures, we may see some others in which Degas plays variations on the principles or ideas involved. *Portraits in an Office* (*Figure 9*), or as it has also been called, *The Cotton Market, New Orleans*, was painted in 1873 during Degas's visit to relatives in New Orleans. His mother was a native of that city, and the picture shows her brother, Degas's

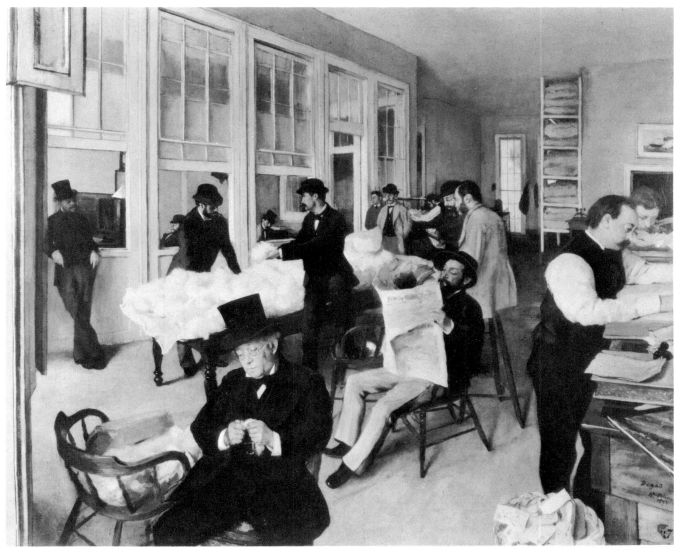

Figure 9

17

uncle Michel Musson, seated in the foreground testing a sample of cotton fiber while clerks and buyers go about their business in the room behind him. Degas repeats some of the compositional devices of the *Rehearsal*, painted the year before. The vacant chair in the foreground, for instance, serves much the same function in both arrangements. But Degas goes farther in giving the impression of reproducing this even more ordinary scene as if the participants were unaware of the painter-spectator. *Portraits in an Office* is not only a snapshot but a candid-camera composition, an effect emphasized by the cutting off of parts of the figures and desks at the right, as well as the legs, from the knees down, of the principal figure, Musson. The eccentric angle of vision, from above and to one side, is more marked than in the *Rehearsal*, increasing the separation of observer and subject. Although we see the office and the men in it at close range, the bird's-eye view convinces us that the participants are not posed but that we have caught them in a chance aspect of their daily routine, leaving us free to observe with the full conviction that their reality is total.

Degas's passion as a draughtsman was the study of momentary attitudes of maximum expressiveness. He lies in wait for the gesture, the stance, the turn of a head, that characterizes an individual as to occupation, social status, and even way of thought. Entertainers fascinated him as personalities whose gestures and postures were unusually vivid, but the remarkable thing about his studies of performers is that we are aware of them first as people, and only secondarily as parts of a staged spectacle. The figures in his *Two Café Singers* (Plate J 7) are complete personalities. Degas offers them to us entire; uncannily we feel that we know the timbre of voice, the caliber of the performance, the nature of the song. The few lines describing bones, flesh, hair, and dress not only create two human beings but evoke place and time. Everything counts, and some of the apparently most in-

cidental bits count most. The outward crook of the thumb of the singer to our right is an expressive gesture in itself, telling us as much as the face. Degas has changed its position at least once, emphasizing its projection; the erasure can still be seen, and we must believe that the change was made not for greater factual accuracy but for its expressive value. The thumb is, as a matter of fact, somewhat oversize if we want to be strict about factual accuracy.

Degas is the great draughtsman of impressionism. Only Ingres, and occasionally Daumier in a more closely related way, can equal him in his century. The connection with the classical master is closer than one might think. Ingres the draughtsman (not Ingres the pedant) was Degas's demigod. One of the high points of Degas's youth was a visit to Ingres's studio. Through his wealthy and influential father, Degas had obtained an important Ingres for the Salon of the Exposition Universelle. The owner had previously refused to lend the painting, which Ingres wanted very much to show, and the old painter granted young Degas an interview as a gesture of thanks. Degas was twenty-one and his ambition was to study under Ingres, but the old master was accepting no pupils. He told Degas to "draw lines, many lines." The lines of *Two Café Singers*, drawn many years later, seem to bear little relationship to Ingres's dulcet lines, but they are in the tradition of solid draughtsmanship in which knowing description of the human body is modified according to the expressive needs of the artist.

Degas's role as a leader in the formation of the impressionist group and its preservation during the intramural squabbles that soon beset it is a most creditable one. He had nothing to gain, financially or as to reputation. Not only was he wealthy but he actually disliked to sell pictures, as the other members hoped to do through the group shows. He had been regularly accepted in the Salon, and his family was influential enough to give him a

Figure 10

head start in a conventional career. Furthermore, Degas was not of a nature that would draw him naturally into group projects, especially those involving Bohemian types at odds with his own aristocratic inclination. He was extremely reserved, almost secretive, and sometimes cantankerous.

Degas identified himself with the new painting because he believed in it. He quarreled with the other organizing members, insisted upon the inclusion of some painters they disliked (usually rather conservative or popular artists who might serve as decoys to the public), and he had no sympathy with painting out of doors, claiming that the smell of country air made him sick. The closest he ever came to the open fields was the race track. But he recognized Monet and the other impressionists as the important painters of the time. He saw too that in spite of all differences he was basically one of them because he was interested in painting things around him in appropriate ways, instead of conventional subjects according to formula.

Degas was a wit with a sharp tongue. He could annihilate an adversary with a phrase, and he never hesitated to do so. A thousand stories represent him as a mild eccentric, a woman hater, and an amusing cynic. But picture after picture shows us instead a sensitively responsive man with deep human sympathies; an artist who might indeed record with merciless objectivity a pair of aging prostitutes at a sidewalk café, but who, on the other hand, could paint pictures like the portrait of his blind cousin, Estelle Musson (Plate J 8).

Estelle was also Degas's sister-in-law, the wife of his younger brother, René, who had gone to New Orleans to enter the family's cotton business there. The portrait, like the scene in Michel Musson's office, was painted during Degas's visit to America. He had always had a particular affection for René, and by the evidence of the portrait he extended this feeling to Estelle. Poignant associations make the picture hard to describe without

falling into sentimental presumptions. But even if we do not know that the young woman is blind, we feel her isolation as she sits so patiently against a wall that is suggestively blank and faces a light in which there is no suggestion that she sees anything.

Degas too became blind, or nearly so, in his last years. For some time he had done occasional bits of sculpture. As early as 1880-81 he had completed his only large piece (one other, a portrait, was lost in casting) of a ballet "rat," a young dancer in training (*Figure 10*). It is of approximately the same date as the *Two Café Singers* and has a similar quality, for it is as much a three-dimensional drawing as it is a piece of sculpture. The *tutu* (ballet skirt), in real tarlaton, is momentarily distracting. Yet it is impossible to imagine how Degas could have represented it in bronze without reducing the startling impression of actuality created by the rest of the statue.

As his sight failed Degas turned more and more to sculpture, still, essentially, as a draughtsman for whom there had never been a distinction between line and mass. Where his dim eyes could perceive only the coarsest lines on paper, they could discern the silhouettes of solid forms, and what his eyes could not see his hands could tell him. He left some 150 small studies, the majority of them female nudes—dancers practicing their steps, women sponging or scratching themselves, lying in tubs, kneeling, walking.

Manet and Impressionism

Degas came closest to finding an intimate friend in Manet, since the two men shared a background of wealth and social amenity and, it must be admitted, a suspicious attitude toward the less gracious ways of living. But while Degas worked with the impressionists as a matter of faith, Manet held himself aloof in spite of his position as their mentor at the Café Guerbois during their formative years. He was only a few years older than they (only

Figure 11

two years older than Degas, and even two years younger than Pissarro, who eventually became the dean of impressionism), but as the painter of *The Picnic* and *Olympia* he was their martyr as well as their elder statesman. Actually, Manet seems not to have cared much for their company. He was polite, but he found his few friends in his own social circle, barricading himself behind a formal cordiality. He refused to join the impressionists as an exhibiting group.

Manet's goal was simple: election to the Academy. He was determined to conquer the Salon; not, like Renoir, because he saw Salon success as a form of security, but because he continued to think of it as the ultimate in prestige. He continued to submit his pictures, year after year; sometimes they were accepted; twice, even, he had Salon successes. But the balance was overwhelmingly humiliating, with

unreasonable rejections and bitter attacks on the pictures that were accepted. Two years before his death an old friend, Antonin Proust, was appointed Minister of Fine Arts and forced Manet's election to the Legion of Honor with a medal. But Manet was too ill to enjoy the tardy and dubious award. He died in 1883 and before a year had gone by a memorial show was held at the École des Beaux Arts, the Academy's fortress.

This occurred only shortly before the impressionists' last group show of 1886. Over the years Manet had been affected by impressionist developments, even though he had refused to take part in the shows. For a while he had resisted the appeal of outdoor painting, but had been won over after watching Monet paint at Argenteuil, one of the impressionists' favorite spots on the Seine. In 1874, the year of the first show, he painted *Boating* (Portfolio 2, Plate 23, and *Figure 14*), and from time to time he did other outdoor subjects. He never became wholeheartedly an outdoor painter, but his color freshened and his brush increased in freedom at least partially because of the experience. The change is apparent if we compare a picture of 1877, *Skating* (Plate J9), with *Olympia*. Like *Olympia*, *Skating* is a portrait of a courtesan, this time a fashionable one whom Manet considered the perfect example of her type. (She was Henriette Hauser, the model for Zola's *Nana*.) *Olympia* is presented to us as if in a flash of instant vision, but the model and her attendant maid are carefully posed. In *Skating* the pose is more casual, as if the subject has paused for just a moment at Manet's request, while most of the accompanying figures continue their activity unaware. A man at the extreme left is bisected by the margin, a favorite device of Degas's, of course, while the young woman at background right happens to look up as the "camera" clicks. Her face, hat and veil, and the whirling skaters behind her are described in flashing strokes.

We have seen the slightly later portrait of George Moore (Portfolio 10, Plate 113) in which Manet pushed his brilliant impressionistic suggestion even further than he did in *Skating*. But his last major picture, *The Bar at the Folies Bergère* (*Figure 11*), indicates that he shared the general uneasiness with the course impressionism had followed and that if he had lived—he was just turning fifty when he painted *The Bar at the Folies Bergère*—he would have entered a new period with increased attention to formal composition and solidly defined volumes. The background, a large mirror reflecting the crowded audience, is an impressionist play of color from which an occasional figure, holding opera glasses or reading a program, emerges. But the barmaid is as boldly and as sharply defined as *Olympia*, while the composition is more severely ordered than any other of Manet's by the triangular form of the central figure and the structural

Figure 12

geometry of insistent verticals and horizontals.

The Bar at the Folies Bergère was painted with great difficulty. Manet was increasingly ill; locomotor ataxia made each hour's work anguishing. But this last picture is the work of an artist in midstream of his creative powers, who had begun to explore in a direction prophetic of geometrical abstraction.

Morisot and Cassatt

Impressionism produced two exceptional woman painters, Berthe Morisot (1841–1895) and Mary Cassatt (1845–1926). It may be unfair to put a painter who happens to be a woman in a special category, but it is somehow even less flattering to say of her that she "paints with the vigor of a man." Both Morisot, a Frenchwoman, and Cassatt, an American, were artists whose work held special attraction and displayed individual character precisely because it expressed a feminine point of view towards the world.

And both women had an admirably feminine loyalty to the painters who most influenced them, respectively Manet and Degas.

Morisot was Manet's sister-in-law. She admired him and was much influenced by his style, but her first interest in painting did not stem from this connection. She had been a pupil of Corot, and she was a granddaughter of Fragonard, whose playful art (Portfolio G, *Figures 6, 7*) has its own feminine quality. Berthe Morisot was a deft painter and one demanding such adjectives as charming, delightful, and delicate, which may connote lack of substance. But if ever she lacks substance, it is not a substance she tried for and failed to achieve. *In the Dining Room* (Plate J 10), a portrait of her maid, is consummately charming, delightful, and delicate—and certainly it is deft. It might almost be an exceptionally sparkling Manet, except that it has a briskness and here and there a thinness not typical of her brother-in-law's painting. The maid, with her pretty face featured by two dots for eyes and a little stroke of red for the mouth, can be compared with the background female figure in *Skating* for the all but imitative similarity of technique, and contrasted with it for the difference between Manet's force and Morisot's daintiness.

Morisot was the hardest worker in the impressionist cause and its most faithful adherent, forswearing Salon exhibition and appearing in all but one of the group shows. She took on chores of organization that no one else would spare time for, soothed hurt feelings, placated outraged members, and did a great deal of good by propagandizing for the rebels among her well-placed friends. With all this she combined matrimony and motherhood. (Her one failure to exhibit with the group was during pregnancy.) Her letters are as interesting as her painting, or even more so; her comments on her fellow artists and their work have the startling vividness of good gossip combined with informal history and sound criticism.

Mary Cassatt, the daughter of a wealthy Pennsylvania family, chose a career against her family's wishes without the impedimenta of husband and children. She managed to associate professionally with Parisian rebels while maintaining an active social life of irreproachable conventionality on both sides of the Atlantic at a time when conventions were more demanding than nowadays.

If Mary Cassatt had done nothing else, she would be an important figure in American art because she interested her wealthy American friends in impressionist painting and helped them form collections that are now the envy of the world and, in retrospect, something of a rebuke to the French. Mr. and Mrs. H. O. Havemeyer were two such friends, and their collection, now in the Metropolitan Museum, is in itself a magnificent museum of latter nineteenth-century painting and sculpture.

Before she came under the influence of the impressionists, Mary Cassatt exhibited in two Salons, showing sound but not very interesting pictures that held echoes of Velazquez and Caravaggio. But when she came into contact with impressionism, she was immediately responsive to it. Her last Salon acceptance coincided with the first of the group shows. Degas became her mentor, and in 1879 she identified herself with the society, exhibiting that year and in all but one of the subsequent shows. The youngest of the group, she lived to the age of eighty-one and witnessed the triumph of the school of painting she had done so much to further, had the satisfaction of being recognized as America's foremost woman painter, a position she still holds, and was decorated by the government of her second country, France.

Cassatt's painting justifies her reputation, but she made her most individual contribution with her prints. These are not merely drawings translated into another medium but works of art whose character is wholly determined by the medium. In this sense she is one of the first modern printmakers. Printmaking occupied many of the impressionists, and their painting was influenced by Japanese woodblocks, where the tilted perspective used by Degas and others was found. With the Japanese as her models Cassatt developed a style of succinct contours and flat, ornamental pattern. Her debt to the Japanese as well as her individuality should be apparent to the reader in a comparison of *Maternal Caress* (*Figure 12*) with Harunobu's *Mother and Child with Bird* (Portfolio 10, Plate 119).

Fin de Siècle

As impressionism waned towards the end of the century, it put forth a curious flower in the work of a man young enough to have been the son of the painter he most admired, Degas. This was Henri de Toulouse-Lautrec (1864-1901), heir to one of the oldest titles in France, deformed by crippling accidents during childhood so that he hobbled about with the legs of a dwarf, who turned to the cafés and brothels of Montmartre because he was denied a normal life in his own world. His art is the art of Degas narrowed and sharpened in a milieu of fever and boredom. We have seen him as an observer of society in the *Salon in the Rue des Moulins* (Portfolio 11, Plate 130), as a printmaker in the *Clown* (Portfolio 10, Plate 120), and as a designer of posters in *Aristide Bruant* (Portfolio 5, Plate 60). The relationship between his work and impressionism is demonstrated in one of his very few large and carefully finished pictures, *At the Moulin Rouge* (Plate J 11).

Toulouse-Lautrec's impressionism had very little to do with effects of natural light and atmosphere. His light is gaslight, and it burns in fetid air. His few outdoor pictures, usually portraits painted in the stunted gardens of Montmartre, show the chalky faces of people unaccustomed to the sun; the foliage behind them is an acid green as if nourished by unnatural soil. The slice of life he shows us is sordid and bizarre, but Toulouse-Lautrec never paints sordidness or evil from relish of them, any more than he sentimentalizes or preaches. He does not comment, or at least he seldom appears to; he describes with the eye of a good journalist the most telling details of a situation, and with the drawing of an artist who could summarize his vision of a personality in half a dozen snakelike lines. His vision is more restricted than Degas's because he was content to stay within the limits of a specialized aspect of the human scene, but within these limitations the scene is as complete as it can be from the point of view of one man. If Toulouse-Lautrec did not create a world, he left a unique record of one as it appeared to an individual with an extraordinarily sharp eye, who moved within it as a privileged spectator.

Moulin Rouge shows part of the promenade that surrounded the dance floor of the famous cabaret, a meeting place equally for intellectuals, slummers, Bohemians, and riffraff. The group at the center table are identifiable acquaintances of Toulouse-Lautrec's. Behind them appears his grotesque head; he is accompanied by his cousin and best friend, the lanky Tapié de Celeyran. Adjusting her topknot, back towards us, is La Goulue, a dancer who queened it at the Moulin Rouge until obesity and alcoholism put an end to her career. She is accompanied by a female friend. May Milton, another popular entertainer, appears prominently at the right. The rail between promenade and dance floor cuts across the lower left, separating us from these people and identifying us further with Lautrec's view, in a double sense, of the subject.

Even more emphatically than in Degas, the haphazardly planned composition makes us observers yet nonparticipants. Originally the composition was more conventional, since it did not include the weirdly illuminated face of May Milton. In order to introduce it Lautrec added to his canvas, piecing it out at the right side and at the bottom. Without the added figure the picture loses its strongest point, the clash between the strident chemical blue-green of the shadows on the face and the violently orange hair of the woman seated at the table. These colors vibrate between one another within a scheme of smaller areas of sharp colors lashed by accents of black and purple. The composition may be Lautrec-after-Degas, but the color is Toulouse-Lautrec's own, the color of his world with its artificial stimulations, its excitements, and its ennuis, a shrill world divided between avidity for sensation and indifference to life. We are far removed from the summer idyl of another dance, Renoir's *Dancing at the Moulin de la Galette*.

Whistler

Impressionism was born, flourished, and was abandoned in Paris before it was adopted by painters in other countries. The exception was the man whose portrait of his mother (Portfolio 1, Plate 1) everybody knows, the American James Abbott McNeill Whistler (1834–1903). "Whistler's Mother," properly entitled *Arrangement in Gray and Black*, is also an arrangement of flat geometrical shapes related to Japanese print composition, here adapted to the portrait of an American woman by her son who studied in France and painted, largely, in England.

Having been dismissed from West Point (he failed chemistry), Whistler, like Pissarro, arrived in Paris in 1855, the year of the Exposition Universelle. Before long he knew Courbet, Manet, Monet, Degas, and Fantin-Latour. His picture *The White Girl* (*Figure 13*) was considered particularly offensive when it was shown in the Salon des Refusés. If the moody stare of the subject looks familiar, the explanation is that Whistler admired the Pre-Raphaelites, especially Rossetti, whose circle he soon joined.

Just why Whistler chose to abandon Paris for London at this point is a question no one has answered. Certainly it was not from discouragement, for he loved a good scrap and

Figure 13

for the rest of his life he went out of his way to stir up controversies in England similar to those that arose naturally in France. Across the Channel he devoted himself to shocking Victorian society into an awareness of new standards in art.

Whistler's most spectacular foray into the limelight was his brush with John Ruskin, whose discovery of Turner and support of the Pre-Raphaelites had made him the foremost of England's tiny band of enlightened critics. But his enlightenment stopped short of Whistler's impressionism (partly, perhaps, because his patience gave out before the artist's

25

Figure 14

antics), and he finally broke when confronted with a fantasy called *Falling Rocket: Nocturne in Black and Gold.* The picture was a shower of bright color against a dark background, and it might have pleased Turner, but Ruskin wrote: "I have seen, and heard, much of cockney impudence before now; but never expected to hear a coxcomb ask two hundred guineas for flinging a pot of paint in the public's face." Whistler sued for libel, not because he was outraged by the criticism, but because he was delighted to exercise his showman's knack for getting himself and his theories before the public. He won the suit, with damages of one farthing, and broke poor Ruskin's career. (Whistler himself was almost bankrupted by his legal fees.)

Whistler's theories were somewhat precious, or seem so today, but they are important historically because he propounded the principle of art for art's sake upon which so much contemporary painting is based. We have said that this principle is implied in *Olympia*, and we will have more to say of it in our concluding discussions.

Whistler's soft-edged visions of both real and imaginary subjects place him among the impressionists, although he had little to do with the bright broken color of the Frenchmen. His atmospheric pictures, which he often called "Nocturnes," were rendered in films of muted blues and grays with flecks of yellow for lights. *Falling Rocket* was an unusually bright example; at the other extreme, his canvases might present only a haze of two or three tones fading into one another. In his portraits, including the one of his mother, Whistler was closer to the protoimpressionism of Velazquez than to Manet, Renoir, or Degas, as the portrait of *Miss Cicely Alexander* (*Figure 14*; detail, *Figure 15*) shows. In another costume, Miss Alexander might be an infanta of the Spanish court painted by a student of Velazquez who, by a chronologically impossible chance, had run across a Japanese print. Whistler's etchings, a most important aspect of his art, were discussed in Portfolio 10.

American Postscript

In the United States there was a lively school of impressionist landscape painters during the early years of the twentieth century who had formed an association, "Ten American Painters," in 1898 and have lately been dubbed the "Academy of American Impressionism." Their descendants may still be found painting busily alongside modernists in art colonies throughout the country. Their work is often attractive but discussion of it would

Figure 15

be redundant. One group, however, created an American variation on the French slice-of-life idea to give a picture of New York comparable to the one their forebears had given of Paris, with Daumier as well as Manet and the early work of Monet among their models. These were the "ash-can" painters, so named in derision because they hunted out the alleys, the grubby backyards, the rented rooms, the cheap bars and restaurants of the city along with its avenues and parks in an effort to record typically American aspects of life in a typically American way. Originating as "The Philadelphia Realists" in that city in the 1890s, they migrated to New York about 1900, where they took on their typical character. A bit later,

with some changes in membership, they called themselves "The Eight," but for convenience we may use the descriptive ash-can title to cover the three stages of their history.

The ash-can painters regarded brusque vigor, rough activity, and a happy jumble of optimistic activity as typically American, reflecting these characteristics in techniques that could become merely heavy and careless. But occasionally they went beneath the hectic and flashy surface of city life to discover the poetry that exists in life anywhere, and which may be unusually affecting when it appears unexpectedly in the least poetic environment. As the most typical member of the ash-can school, John Sloan (1871–1951) ran its gamut from

Figure 16

28

broadly, even crudely painted scenes of the Bohemian life in New York's Greenwich Village (the natural habitat of the ash-can painters) to *The Wake of the Ferry* (*Figure 16*), one of the fine expressions of a recurrent theme in pictures of urban life—the moments of reflective isolation that occur within the crowding circumstances and thoughtless routine of day-to-day living. Daumier's *Print Collector* (Portfolio 12, Plate 144) is another example.

Cézanne

The paintings in the first impressionist exhibition included three by a puzzling man named Paul Cézanne (1839–1906). Among the painters who met at the Café Guerbois, Cézanne was an unknown quantity; he was admitted to the show only upon the insistence of Pissarro, that patient man of good will, who was the only one of Cézanne's acquaintances who could stomach for long so difficult a person. For Cézanne was difficult. He was awkward, intense, intolerant, often sullen and suspicious. He remained on the sidelines of the talk around the table, except to deliver occasional violently phrased pronouncements in the exaggerated way of many socially timid people when they state their convictions. He was never easily a member of the group, but Manet once complimented him on a still life, Pissarro found a gentleness in him that was hidden from others, and, above all, Zola, a boyhood friend, sponsored him (the two men were later to quarrel bitterly).

At thirty-five, when the first show was held, Cézanne was still trying to find himself. The son of a wealthy hatmaker-turned-banker of Aix-en-Provence who opposed his interest in art, he had tried to study law. Abandoning this course as hopeless, he had come to Paris to prepare for entrance to the Academy's school. Discouraged by early failures, he returned to Aix-en-Provence and his father's bank. But soon he was back in Paris, carrying on his tortured but determined studies. During the next years he moved back and forth between Paris, Aix, and other small cities where he felt less an outsider than he did in the capital. When we say that he consistently entered pictures for the Salon, we need hardly add that they were consistently rejected.

Cézanne's earliest paintings show the combined influences of Italian baroque masters and Delacroix, interpreted in curious, heavy, groping, awkward—but strong—ways. Under the influence of Courbet he developed a passion for heavy rich pigment, painting sometimes with the palette knife in broad, choppy planes that made his paintings resemble the early stages of sculpture blocked out in stone. His portrait *Man with a Straw Hat* (Plate J 12) has much of this character; the definition of individual planes by strokes of color also holds the germ of his later analysis of color-and-plane relationships that not only transformed his art but redirected the course of painting in a way so far reaching that it can be compared only to Giotto's revolution six hundred years before.

Cézanne's preoccupation with the structure of objects is apparent in even his crudest early efforts, and it is certainly apparent in this powerful head. It is evident even when, working with Pissarro, he painted the pictures that can, by stretching a point, be called impressionist. Even more than Pissarro he refused to sacrifice formal definition to impressionist sparkle. *The House of the Hanged Man* (*La Maison du pendu*, *Figure 17*), which was in the first impressionist exhibition, is impressionist in color, but the broken tints are built up in heavy impasto and are held within the boundaries of the objects represented. It is a strong picture; it defines where impressionism suggests, it is forceful rather than charming. In the unyielding angularities of its major lines, combined with a few curves as solidly built as arches, the compositional scheme anticipates the complicated geometry of Cézanne's later work that, in turn, was a source of cubism and a dozen other experimental movements.

29

Figure 17

Cézanne refused to exhibit in the second impressionist show; in the third, that of 1877, he exhibited sixteen pictures; he did not exhibit again, spending less and less time in Paris until finally he became a recluse in Aix. Where Renoir rejected impressionism to rebuild upon the art of the past, Cézanne rejected it to explore in new directions. At that point he ceased to be part of the movement, and although he was a contemporary of the men we have discussed here, his art belongs with that of the next generation, and of our century.

Color Plates

Figures

(Figure 7) Oil on canvas. Height 27¼''. The Louvre Museum, Paris

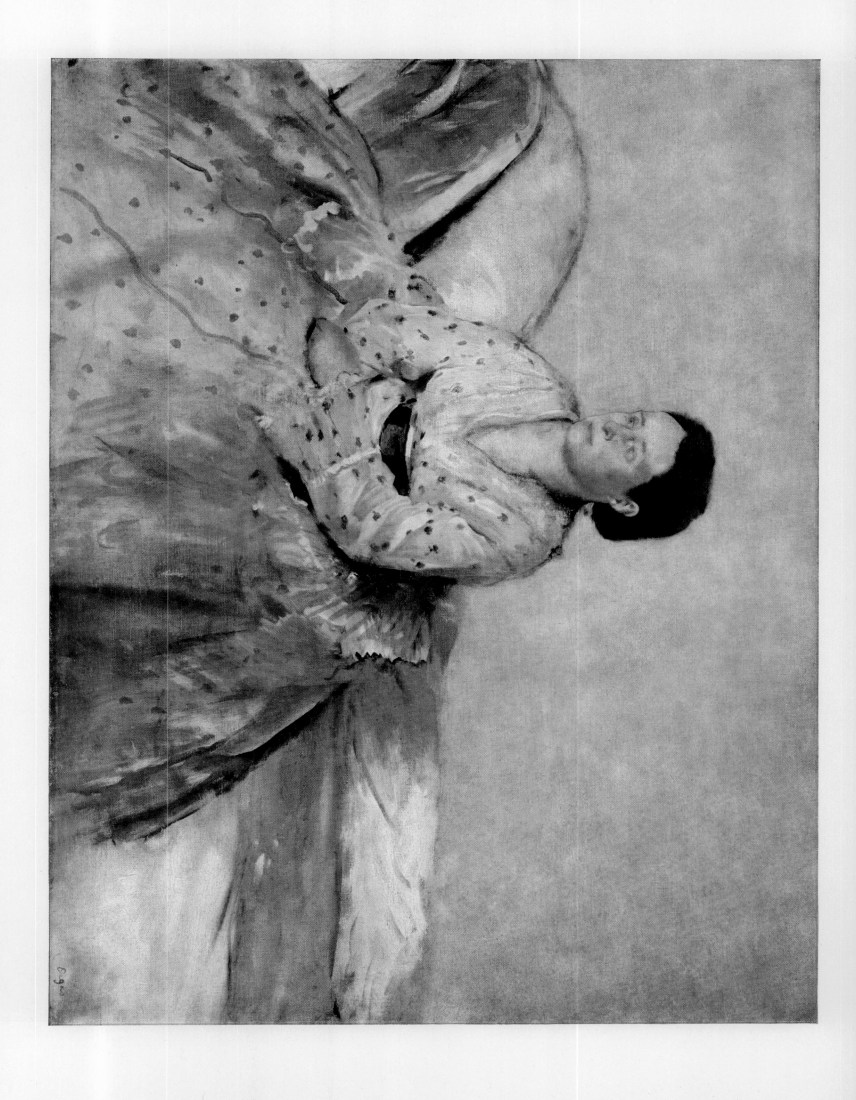

MADAME RENÉ DE GAS (ESTELLE MUSSON) Degas The National Gallery of Art, Washington

ÎLE AUX FLEURS   *Monet*   The Metropolitan Museum of Art

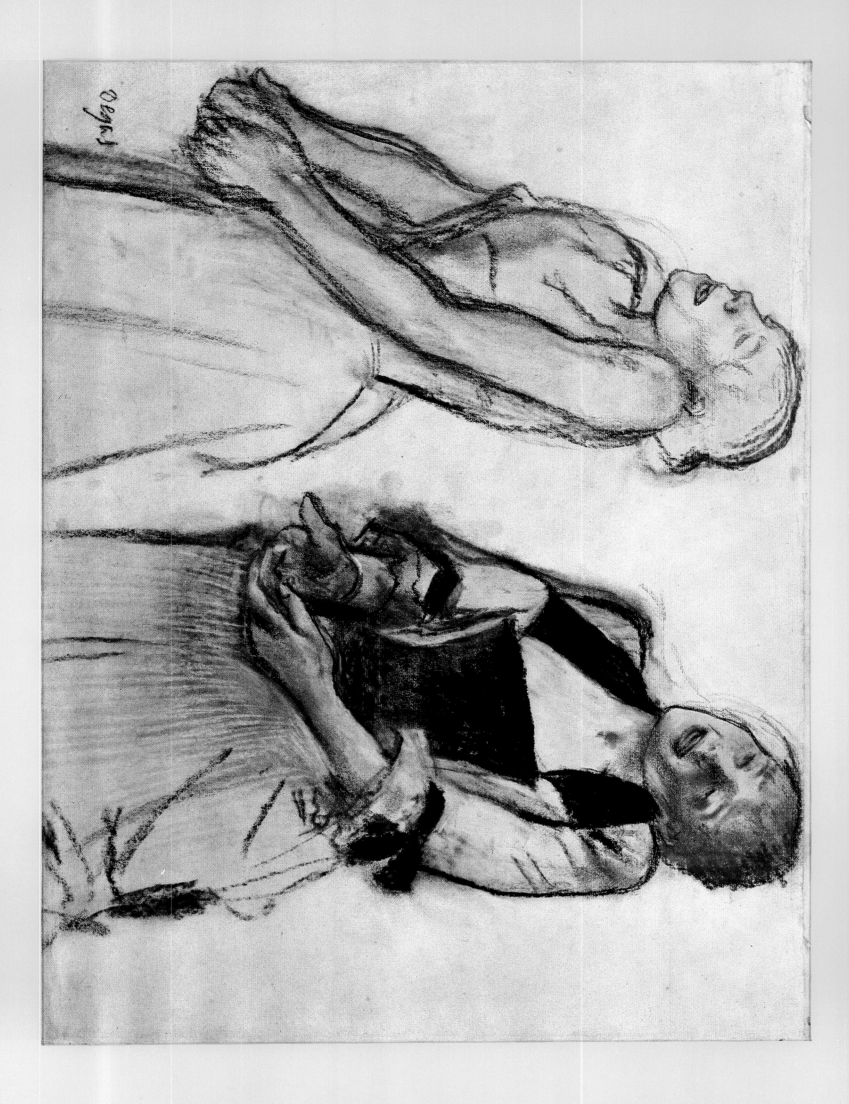

PLATE 16   Detail from BATHERS   Renoir   Tyson Collection, Philadelphia

PLATE 14

THE PONT NEUF   *Pissarro*   Mr. and Mrs. William Coxe Wright, Philadelphia

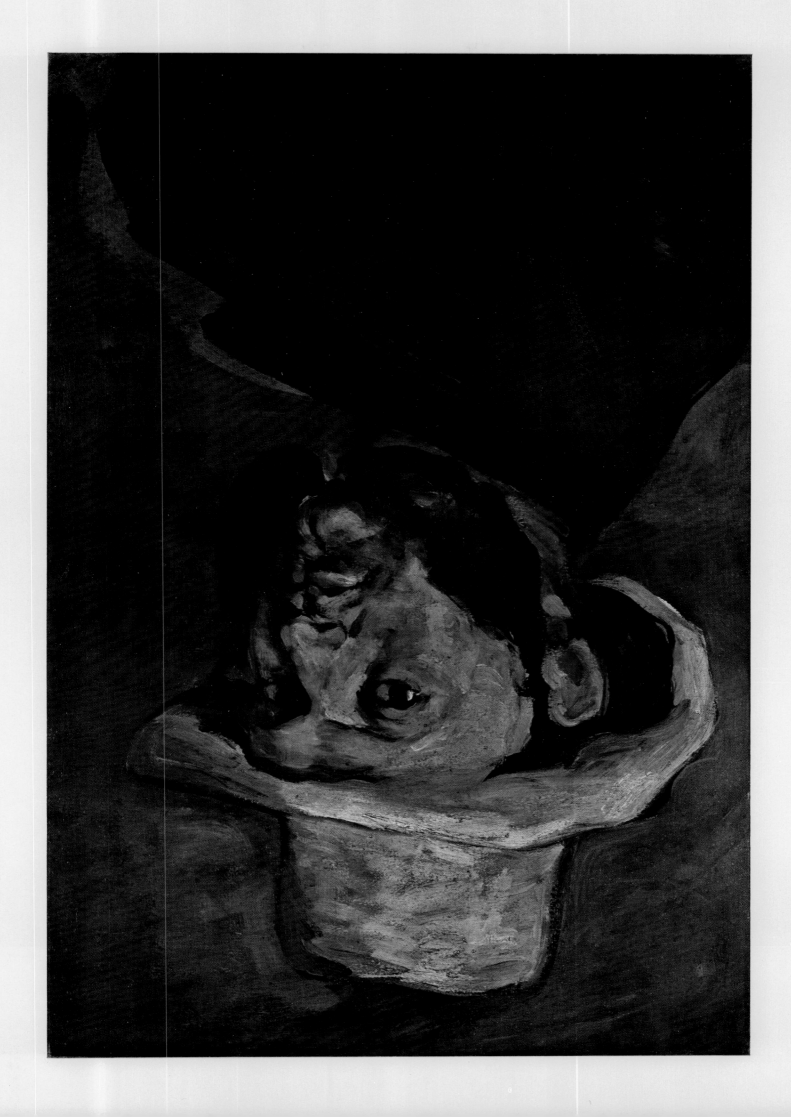